Papatango Theatre Company in
Finborough Theatre present

The World Premiere of the winner of the Papatango New
Writing Prize 2013 in partnership with the Finborough Theatre

UNSCORCHED

by Luke Owen

FINBOROUGH | THEATRE

First performance at the Finborough Theatre: Tuesday, 29 October 2013

UNSCORCHED

by Luke Owen

Cast in order of appearance

Nidge	**John Hodgkinson**
Simon	**Richard Atwill**
Mark	**George Turvey**
Tom	**Ronan Raftery**
Emily	**Eleanor Wyld**

Director	**Justin Audibert**
Designer	**Georgia Lowe**
Lighting Designer	**Joshua Carr**
Sound Designer	**Richard Hammarton**
Production Manager	**Timothy Peacock**
Stage Manager	**Roisin Symes**
Casting Director	**Emily Jones**
Assistant Director	**Jonny Kelly**
Producer	**Chris Foxon**
Assistant Producer	**Jessica Campbell**

The action takes place in the UK, 2013.

The performance lasts approximately 90 minutes.

There will be no interval.

Our patrons are respectfully reminded that, in this intimate theatre, any noise such as rustling programmes, talking or the ringing of mobile phones may distract the actors and your fellow audience-members.

We regret there is no admittance or re-admittance to the auditorium whilst the performance is in progress.

Cast and Creative Team

Richard Atwill | Simon
Productions at the Finborough Theatre include
iWitness (2007), *Captain Oates' Left Sock* (2009) and
Beating Heart Cadaver (2011).

Trained at LAMDA.

Theatre includes *Macbeth* and *Macbett* (Royal
Shakespeare Company); *God in Ruins* (Royal
Shakespeare Company and Soho Theatre); *The
Changing Room* (Royal Court Theatre); *Ravenhill for
Breakfast* (Traverse Theatre, Edinburgh); *The Roman
Bath* (Arcola Theatre and National Theatre Bulgaria);
Beyond the Pale (Southwark Playhouse); *The
Adventure* (Pleasance Edinburgh and Royal Exchange
Theatre, Manchester); *Coalition* (Theatre503); *The Merchant of Venice* (Hazlitt
Theatre, Maidstone); *Seawall* (Acre Theatre, Israel); *Swing* and *Invisible Storms*
(Cock Tavern); *Roots* (Clwyd Theatr Cymru); and *Potted Potter* (Little Schubert
Theatre, New York).

Film includes *Best, Canvas* and *The Monkey Cage*.

Television includes *Doctors* and *Il Spettacolo Di Ricky E Lucy*.

John Hodgkinson | Nidge
Productions at the Finborough Theatre include the
staged reading of *Photos of You Sleeping* as part of
the 2012 Papatango New Writing Prize (2012).

Theatre includes *A Walk On Part* (Live Theatre
Newcastle, Soho Theatre and Arts Theatre); *The
Seagull* (National Theatre); *Onassis* (West End);
London Assurance (Chichester Festival Theatre and
West End); *Behud* (Soho Theatre); *The Winter's
Tale* (Headlong); *Absurdia* and *The Front Page*
(Donmar Warehouse); *The Eleventh Capital* (Royal
Court Theatre); *Alice in Wonderland, Alice Through
the Looking Glass, Love's Labour's Lost, A Jovial
Crew, The Beggar's Opera, The Winter's Tale, Dr
Jekyll and Mr Hyde, The Pretenders, Richard II, Edward II* and *The Comedy
of Errors* (Royal Shakespeare Company); *His Dark Materials, Uncle Vanya,
Neville's Island* and *The Hare Trilogy* (Birmingham Rep); *Aristo, Love's
Labour's Lost* and *The Visit* (Chichester Festival Theatre); *Hapgood*
(Birmingham Rep and West Yorkshire Playhouse); *The Taming of the Shrew,
A Midsummer Night's Dream, The Two Gentlemen of Verona, Romeo and
Juliet, As You Like It* and *Oh! What a Lovely War* (Open Air Theatre, Regent's
Park); *A Journey to London* (Orange Tree Theatre, Richmond); *I Have Been
Here Before* (Watford Palace Theatre); *Arcadia* (Bristol Old Vic); *Events While
Guarding the Bofors Gun* and *Leocadia* (Royal Shakespeare Company
Festival); *Cardboard City* (National Tour); *Le Bourgeois Gentilhomme*
(Edinburgh Festival); and *Good Morning Bill* (Scala Theatre, Stockholm).

Film includes *Skyfall, Heart of Lightness, Leave to Remain, Thunderpants,
Firelight* and *Whatever Happened to Harold Smith?*

Television includes *Big Bad World, The Escape Artist, Whitechapel, Silk, Holby City, Criminal Justice, Fall Out, Heartbeat, Broken News, Doctors, Brief Encounters, Peep Show, EastEnders, My Family, The Lee Evans Show, Chambers, The Bill, The Estate Agents, People Like Us, Kiss Me Kate, The Peter Principle, Pure Wickedness, Boyz Unlimited, Then, Keeping Mum, Duck Patrol, Dad, Sometime Never* and *Inside Victor Lewis Smith*.

Ronan Raftery | Tom
Trained at RADA.

Theatre includes *Juno and the Paycock* (National Theatre); *A View from the Bridge* (Royal Exchange Theatre, Manchester); *Brighton Beach Memoirs* (Watford Palace Theatre); and *The Shawshank Redemption* (West End).

Film includes *Captain America* and *Death of a Superhero*.

Television includes *Fresh Meat, Moone Boy, Crossing Lines* and *Doctors*.

Radio includes *Ulysses*.

George Turvey | Mark
Theatre includes the title role in *Batman Live* (World Arena Tour); *The Importance of Being Earnest* (Theatre Royal Bath and West End); *Romeo and Juliet* (Middle Temple Hall); *Christmas Reloaded* (Old Red Lion Theatre); and *Potentials* (Tristan Bates Theatre).

Television includes *Which is Witch?*

Eleanor Wyld | Emily
Productions at the Finborough Theatre include *Rigor Mortis* as part of the 2011 Papatango New Writing Prize (2011).

Trained at Guildhall School of Music and Drama.

Theatre includes *Dances of Death* (Gate Theatre); *The Astronaut's Chair* (Theatre Royal Plymouth); *Shiverman* (Theatre503); *His Teeth* (Only Connect); *Antigone* (Southwark Playhouse); and *The Deep Blue Sea* (West Yorkshire Playhouse).

Television includes *Misfits, Black Mirror: The National Anthem, Casualty, Honest, You Can Choose Your Friends* and *Coronation Street*.

Film includes *Bonobo, Johnny English Reborn, Freestyle* and *The Manual*.

Luke Owen | Playwright

Luke was born in 1982, grew up in Woking and now lives in Norwich, where he works as an actor and copywriter. He is a graduate of the University of East Anglia, where he took a BA in English and Drama before graduating from the acclaimed MA course in Creative Writing.

He was a member of the Royal Court Theatre Young Writers' Programme.

Justin Audibert | Director

Justin was the recipient of the 2012 Leverhulme Award for Emerging Directors and was Resident Director at the Finborough Theatre and the National Theatre Studio. He is Artistic Associate of HighTide Festival Theatre, Associate Director for Red Ladder and Associate of Told by an Idiot.

Recent directing includes *A Season in the Congo: Parallel Project* (Clare Theatre at The Young Vic); *Wrong 'Un* (Red Ladder); *Gruesome Playground Injuries* (Gate Theatre); *The Tempest* (Royal Shakespeare Company – Shakespeare in a Suitcase); *Future Regrets* (Royal Shakespeare Company at the Live Theatre, Newcastle); *Mojo* (Royal Shakespeare Company at the Hampstead Downstairs); *Front* (RADA Festival); and *Company Along the Mile* (West Yorkshire Playhouse, The Lowry, Manchester, and Arcola Theatre).

As an Assistant Director, he has worked with Greg Doran, Paul Hunter, Lucy Bailey, David Farr, Rachel Kavanaugh and Sarah Esdaile.

In 2012, he was the Acting Coach for the finalists of BBC 2's *Shakespeare Off By Heart*.

Justin trained on the Birkbeck MFA in Theatre Directing.

Georgia Lowe | Designer

Productions at the Finborough Theatre include *Fanny and Faggot* (2007), *Follow* (2008), *Fog* (2012), *Blue Surge* (2012) and *Facts* (2013).

Other theatre includes *The Ruling Class* (English Theatre Frankfurt); *Commonwealth* (Almeida Projects); *Lift* and *Shallow Slumber* (Soho Theatre); *Ignorance* (Hampstead Downstairs); *Pericles* and *Song of Songs* (Royal Shakespeare Company); *Say it with Flowers* (Sherman Cymru, Cardiff); *Acis and Galatea* and *Susanna* (Iford Arts); *After the Rainfall* (Curious Directive); *The Dark Side of Love* (Royal Shakespeare Company and LIFT for the World Shakespeare Festival); *Drowning on Dry Land* (Jermyn Street Theatre); *Amphibians* (Bridewell Theatre); *Return to Silence* (Pleasance London); *Legacy Falls* (New Players Theatre); *Promise* (Arts Educational Schools); *Departure Lounge* (Waterloo East Theatre); *Whispering Happiness* (Tristan Bates Theatre); and *I Am Montana* (Arcola Theatre Studio).

Georgia was a Linbury Prize for Stage Design Finalist 2011 and was shortlisted for The Jocelyn Herbert Award 2011.

Georgia was Trainee Designer for the Royal Shakespeare Company from 2011–12.

Joshua Carr | Lighting Designer
Productions at the Finborough Theatre include *The Northerners* (2010).

Trained at RADA.

Theatre includes *As You Like It* (International Tour); *The Love Girl and the Innocent* and *Port Authority* (Southwark Playhouse); *Yellow Face* (Park Theatre); *Mudlarks* (HighTide Festival Theatre and Theatre503); *Stage Fright* (Theatre Royal Bury St Edmunds); *Amygdala* (The Print Room); *All My Sons* and *The Miser* (Watermill Theatre, Newbury); *Le Gateau Chocolat: Black* (National Tour); *Jekyll and Hyde* (Edinburgh Festival and Southwark Playhouse); *The Song of Deborah* (The Lowry, Manchester); *House of Cards* (Kensington Palace); *Mansfield Park* (National Tour); *The President and the Pakistani* (Waterloo East Theatre); *One Hour Only* (Old Vic New Voices); *Dick Whittington* (Gatehouse Theatre, Stafford); *His Teeth* (Only Connect); *Love of a Nightingale, The Threepenny Opera, Antigone* and *A Clockwork Orange* (Theatro Technis and Edinburgh Festival); *The Shape of Things* (Soho Gallery); *Breathing Corpses* (Theatre Delicatessen); and *Billy Elliot* and *Cinderella* (Young Actors Theatre).

Theatre as Associate Lighting Designer includes Roundabout Season: *One Day When We Were Young, Lungs* and *The Sound of Heavy Rain* (Paines Plough and Sheffield Theatres); and *The Maddening Rain* (New York).

Theatre as Assistant Lighting Designer includes *Playing the Games* (Criterion Theatre); *Lake Boat and Prairie du Chien* (Arcola Theatre); *Lidless* (Trafalgar Studios); *Portobello* (Edinburgh Festival); *Rose* (Pleasance Edinburgh); and *Ditch* (Old Vic Tunnels).

Richard Hammarton | Sound Designer
Theatre includes *Sizwe Bansi is Dead* and *Six Characters Looking for an Author* (Young Vic); *The Mountaintop* (Theatre503 and Trafalgar Studios); *The Taming of the Shrew* (Shakespeare's Globe); *Brilliant Adventures, Edward II* and *Dr Faustus* (Royal Exchange Theatre, Manchester); *Speaking in Tongues* (Duke of York's Theatre); *A Raisin in the Sun* (Lyric Theatre Hammersmith and National Tour); *I Know How I Feel About Eve* (Hampstead Downstairs); *The Last Summer* (Gate Theatre, Dublin); *Mudlarks* (HighTide Festival, Theatre503 and Bush Theatre); *Ghosts* (Duchess Theatre); *The Pitchfork Disney* (Arcola Theatre); *Judgement Day* (The Print Room); *Same Same, Little Baby Jesus* and *Fixer* (Ovalhouse); *Cheese* (Fanshen Theatre); *An Inspector Calls* (Theatre by the Lake, Keswick); *What Happens in the Winter* (Upswing); *Persuasion, The Constant Wife, Les Liaisons Dangereuses, Arsenic and Old Lace, The Real Thing* and *People at Sea* (Salisbury Playhouse); *Platform* (Old Vic Tunnels); *Pride and Prejudice* (Theatre Royal Bath and National Tour); *The Shooky, Steve Nallon's Christmas Carol* and *Dealer's Choice* (Birmingham Rep); *Hello and Goodbye* and *Some Kind of Bliss* (Trafalgar Studios); *Breakfast with Mugabe* (Theatre Royal Bath); *Someone Who'll Watch Over Me* (Theatre Royal Northampton); *Inches Apart, Ship of Fools, Natural Selection* and *Salt Meets Wound* (Theatre503); and *Blowing* (National Tour).

Film includes *The Pier, First the Worst, A Neutral Corner, Snow, The Button* and *Raptured*.

Television includes *Agatha Christie's Marple, No Win No Fee, Sex 'n' Death, Wipeout, The Ship, Konigsspitz, K2* and *The Fisherman's Wife*.

Orchestration includes *Agatha Christie's Marple, Primeval, Dracula, Jericho, If I Had You, A History of Britain, Silent Witness, Dalziel and Pascoe, Alice Through the Looking Glass, The Nine Lives of Tomas Katz* and *Scenes of a Sexual Nature*.

Interactive work includes pieces at the Foundling Museum, *Moore Outside* at Tate Britain, *You Shall Go to the Ball* at Royal Opera House and *Light* at BAC.

Timothy Peacock | Production Manager
Trained at Guildhall School of Music and Drama.

Theatre as Production Manager includes *Under the Eiderdown* and *Dalston Land of Kids* (Punchdrunk Enrichment); *Anything Goes* and *My Fair Lady* (Kilworth House Theatre); *The Imperfect Pearl* (Whitehouse Productions and Mark Latimer); *Falstaff* (Opera Berbiguieres); and *Dance – Make Your Move* (British Red Cross).

Theatre as Draughtsman includes *Robbie Williams – Take the Crown* (National Tour); *The Village Bike* (Crucible Theatre, Sheffield); *Gravity* (Birmingham Rep) and *Twelfth Night* and *Nicholas Nickleby* (Silk Street Theatre).

Roisin Symes | Stage Manager
Productions at the Finborough Theatre include *Rigor Mortis* (2011) as part of The 2011 Papatango New Writing Prize (2011), and *Pack* (2012), the 2012 Papatango New Writing Prize winner.

Trained at LAMDA.

Theatre includes *The Madwoman Of Chaillot* (Cockpit Theatre); *The Magpies* and *The Wolves* (Tristan Bates Theatre); *Orlando* (BAC); *The Matchgirls* (Wilton's Music Hall); and *Many Moons* (Theatre503).

Emily Jones | Casting Director
Theatre includes *As You Like It* and *Richard III* (Changeling Theatre) and *World Enough and Time* (Dalston Bunker).

Theatre as assistant to Ginny Schiller includes *1984* (Headlong); *Relative Values* (Theatre Royal Bath); *Scenes from a Marriage* (St James Theatre); *A Day in the Death of Joe Egg* and *Ghosts* (Rose Theatre, Kingston); and *Pride and Prejudice* (Open Air Theatre, Regent's Park).

Film includes *Limbo* and *Ibiza Undead*.

Jonny Kelly | Assistant Director
Productions at the Finborough Theatre include Assistant Stage Manager on *I Didn't Always Live Here* (2013).

Trained at East 15.

Theatre as director includes *Sparks Will Fly* (Olympic Ceremonies) and *Awful Weather* (Clifftown Theatre, Southend).

Theatre as an actor includes *Happee* (Roundhouse); *Retz* (Shoreditch Town Hall); *Bush Bazaar* (Bush Theatre) and *Under Milk Wood* (Edinburgh Festival).

Jonny is an associate of Attic Theatre Company.

Chris Foxon | Producer
Productions at the Finborough Theatre include *The Fear of Breathing* (2012), which will premiere in a new production at the Akasaka Red Theatre, Tokyo, in November 2013, *Vibrant – A Festival of Finborough Playwrights* (2012), The 2012 Papatango New Writing Prize (2012) and *I Didn't Always Live Here* (2013).

Read English at Oxford University and trained at the Central School of Speech and Drama on an AHRC Scholarship.

Other productions include *Happy New* (Trafalgar Studios); *Old Vic New Voices 24 Hour Plays* (The Old Vic); *The Madness of George III* (Oxford Playhouse); *Tejas Verdes* (Edinburgh Festival); and the forthcoming *The Keepers of Infinite Space* (Park Theatre).

Theatre as Assistant Producer includes *On the Threshing Floor* (Hampstead Theatre); 'Endless Poem' as part of *Rio Occupation London* (BAC, People's Palace Projects and HighTide Festival Theatre); and *Mudlarks* (HighTide Festival Theatre, Theatre503 and Bush Theatre).

Chris is the producer of Papatango Theatre Company and was an assessor for the 2013 T.S. Eliot Commissions with the Old Vic Theatre.

Jessica Campbell | Assistant Producer
Jessica read English at Oxford University.

Theatre as producer includes *Bloody Poetry* (Keble O'Reilly Theatre) and *Mephisto* (Oxford Playhouse), which transferred to the International Student Drama Festival 2013, *The State Vs John Hayes* (Hen & Chickens Theatre and Edinburgh Festival); and *The Comedy of Errors* (Southwark Playhouse, Yvonne Arnaud Theatre, Guildford, and the Tokyo Metropolitan Theatre, Japan).

Production Acknowledgements

Rehearsal Space | **The Workspace Group**

Production Photography | **Richard Davenport**

Special thanks to the Internet Watch Foundation, Sharon Clarke at the Bristol Old Vic, Sarah Robinson and Rebecca Goodenough for their expertise on child protection, Hilary Best, Hannah Jenner, Arts Council England, the Boris Karloff Charitable Foundation and Airfix.

Unscorched was developed by Papatango Theatre Company at the Bristol Old Vic with the following cast:

Jack Ashton | Oliver Llewellyn-Jenkins | Hannah Miller | Josephine Rattigan

Airfix have provided sponsorship of the models used in the play. For more information go to www.airfix.com or www.facebook.com/officialairfix

Papatango Theatre Company was founded in 2007 to find the best and brightest new writing in the UK with an absolute commitment to bringing this work to the stage.

Papatango have produced or developed new plays in venues including Bristol Old Vic, the Tristan Bates Theatre, the Old Red Lion Theatre, the Finborough Theatre and the Pleasance London, and our discoveries have been produced in many countries worldwide.

The Papatango New Writing Prize was launched in 2009, guaranteeing its winner a full four-week production and publication by Nick Hern Books. The Papatango New Writing Prize is unique in UK theatre – no other new writing competition for full-length plays in the UK absolutely guarantees a full production.

This reflects the company's mission to champion the best new talent and launch brilliant new theatre-makers with the greatest possible impact. Since 2011, the Papatango New Writing Prize has been in partnership with the Finborough Theatre.

Previous winners of the Papatango New Writing Prize include Dawn King's *Foxfinder*, which was one of the Independent's Top Five Plays of the Year, won playwright Dawn King the OffWestEnd Award for Most Promising Playwright and a prestigious Pearson Award bursary through the Finborough Theatre, won the Critics' Circle Most Promising Newcomer Award for director Blanche McIntyre, and was nominated for OffWestEnd Awards for Best New Play and Best Male Performance.

Foxfinder has since been produced in Greece, Sweden, the USA, Australia and Iceland. Dawn and Blanche are now collaborating on the national tour of *Ciphers* with Out of Joint Theatre Company.

2012 prize-winner *Pack* by Louise Monaghan was described by Michael Billington in the *Guardian* as 'knock[ing] spots off much of the new writing I have seen'. Louise has since developed work with Octagon Theatre Bolton and the BBC, while Tom Morton-Smith, writer of our runner-up in the same year, is now under commission to the RSC.

The first winner of the prize, Dominic Mitchell, recently received huge acclaim for his BBC series *In the Flesh*, having been discovered and championed by Papatango who produced *Potentials*, his debut show.

Papatango support not only brilliant new writers and directors but develop the best creative talent in all disciplines. Actors who have worked with the company include Tessa Peake-Jones, Paula Wilcox, John Hodgkinson, Cyril Nri, Angela Lonsdale, Tom Byam Shaw, Sarah Smart, Amita Dhiri, Denise Black, Gyuri Sarossy and Kathryn Drysdale. Designers include James Perkins, Gary Bowman and George Dennis.

Our Assistant Director in 2011, Cathal Cleary, went on to win the JMK Award for Young Directors the following year, and our former Associate Director Bruce Guthrie has gone on to direct in the West End and internationally.

Supported using public funding by
ARTS COUNCIL
LOTTERY FUNDED **ENGLAND**

2013 Papatango New Writing Prize
Unscorched was selected from over 500 entries. It was judged by the four members of Papatango (George Turvey, Chris Foxon, Sam Donovan and Matt Roberts), Neil McPherson, Artistic Director of the Finborough Theatre, Francis Grin, Literary Manager of the Finborough Theatre, and Reen Polonsky, Senior Reader of the Finborough Theatre.

2014 Papatango New Writing Prize
The winner of the 2014 Papatango New Writing Prize will run from 28 October 2014 presented at the Finborough Theatre. Submissions will be accepted from 1 December 2013. For details on how to enter, please go to www.papatango.co.uk/literary-guidelines/.

Online
For up-to-date news join us on Facebook or Twitter or visit www.papatango.co.uk

FINBOROUGH | THEATRE

VIBRANT **NEW WRITING** | UNIQUE **REDISCOVERIES**

'Audacious and successful... West London's Finborough Theatre is one of the best in the entire world. Its programme of new writing and obscure rediscoveries remains "jaw-droppingly good". ' *Time Out*

'A disproportionately valuable component of the London theatre ecology. Its programme combines new writing and revivals, in selections intelligent and audacious.' *Financial Times*

'The Finborough Theatre, under the artistic direction of Neil McPherson, has been earning a place on the must-visit list with its eclectic, smartly curated slate of new works and neglected masterpieces.' *Vogue*

Founded in 1980, the multi-award-winning Finborough Theatre presents plays and music theatre, concentrated exclusively on vibrant new writing and unique rediscoveries from the 19th and 20th centuries. Behind the scenes, we continue to discover and develop a new generation of theatre-makers – through our Literary team, and our programmes for both interns and Resident Assistant Directors.

Despite remaining completely unsubsidised, the Finborough Theatre has an unparalleled track record of attracting the finest creative talent who go on to become leading voices in British theatre. Under Artistic Director Neil McPherson, it has discovered some of the UK's most exciting new playwrights including Laura Wade, James Graham, Mike Bartlett, Sarah Grochala, Jack Thorne, Simon Vinnicombe, Alexandra Wood, Al Smith, Nicholas de Jongh and Anders Lustgarten; and directors including Blanche McIntyre.

Artists working at the theatre in the 1980s included Clive Barker, Rory Bremner, Nica Burns, Kathy Burke, Ken Campbell, Jane Horrocks and Claire Dowie. In the 1990s, the Finborough Theatre first became known for new writing including Naomi Wallace's first play *The War Boys*; Rachel Weisz in David Farr's *Neville Southall's Washbag*; four plays by Anthony Neilson including *Penetrator* and *The Censor*, both of which transferred to the Royal Court Theatre; and new plays by Richard Bean, Lucinda Coxon, David Eldridge, Tony Marchant and Mark Ravenhill. New writing development included the premieres of modern classics such as Mark Ravenhill's *Shopping and F***king*, Conor McPherson's *This Lime Tree Bower*, Naomi Wallace's *Slaughter City* and Martin McDonagh's *The Pillowman*.

Since 2000, new British plays have included Laura Wade's London debut *Young Emma*, commissioned for the Finborough Theatre; two one-woman shows by Miranda Hart; James Graham's *Albert's Boy* with Victor Spinetti; Sarah Grochala's *S27*; Peter Nichols' *Lingua Franca*, which transferred Off-Broadway; and West End transfers for Joy Wilkinson's *Fair*; Nicholas de Jongh's *Plague Over England*; and Jack Thorne's *Fanny and Faggot*. The late Miriam Karlin made her last stage appearance in *Many Roads to Paradise* in 2008.

UK premieres of foreign plays have included Brad Fraser's *Wolfboy*; Lanford Wilson's *Sympathetic Magic*; Larry Kramer's *The Destiny of Me*; Tennessee Williams' *Something Cloudy, Something Clear*; the English premiere of Robert McLellan's Scots language classic, *Jamie the Saxt*; and three West End transfers – Frank McGuinness' *Gates of Gold* with William Gaunt and John Bennett; Joe DiPietro's *F***ing Men*; and Craig Higginson's *Dream of the Dog* with Dame Janet Suzman.

Rediscoveries of neglected work – most commissioned by the Finborough Theatre – have included the first London revivals of Rolf Hochhuth's *Soldiers* and *The Representative*; both parts of Keith Dewhurst's *Lark Rise to Candleford*; *The Women's War*, an evening of original suffragette plays; *Etta Jenks* with Clarke Peters and Daniela Nardini; Noël Coward's first play, *The Rat Trap*; Charles Wood's *Jingo* with Susannah Harker; Emlyn Williams' *Accolade*; Lennox Robinson's *Drama at Inish* with Celia Imrie and Paul O'Grady; John Van Druten's *London Wall* which transferred to St James' Theatre; and J. B. Priestley's *Cornelius* which transferred to a sell-out Off-Broadway run in New York City.

Music Theatre has included the new (premieres from Grant Olding, Charles Miller, Michael John LaChuisa, Adam Guettel, Andrew Lippa, Paul Scott Goodman, and Adam Gwon's *Ordinary Days* which transferred to the West End) and the old (the UK premiere of Rodgers and Hammerstein's *State Fair* which also transferred to the West End, and the acclaimed 'Celebrating British Music Theatre' series, reviving forgotten British musicals.

The Finborough Theatre won The Stage Fringe Theatre of the Year Award in 2011, London Theatre Reviews' Empty Space Peter Brook Award in 2010 and 2012, the Empty Space Peter Brook Award's Dan Crawford Pub Theatre Award in 2005 and 2008, the Empty Space Peter Brook Mark Marvin Award in 2004, and swept the board with eight awards at the 2012 OffWestEnd Awards including Best Artistic Director and Best Director for the second year running. *Accolade* was named Best Fringe Show of 2011 by *Time Out*. It is the only unsubsidised theatre ever to be awarded the Pearson Playwriting Award bursary eight times. Three bursary holders (Laura Wade, James Graham and Anders Lustgarten) have also won the Catherine Johnson Award for Pearson Best Play.

www.finboroughtheatre.co.uk

FINBOROUGH | THEATRE

VIBRANT **NEW WRITING** | UNIQUE **REDISCOVERIES**

118 Finborough Road, London SW10 9ED
admin@finboroughtheatre.co.uk
www.finboroughtheatre.co.uk

The Finborough Theatre has the support of the Pearson Playwrights' Scheme. Sponsored by Pearson PLC.

The Finborough Theatre is a member of the Independent Theatre Council, Musical Theatre Network UK and The Earl's Court Society www.earlscourtsociety.org.uk

Mailing

Email admin@finboroughtheatre.co.uk or give your details to our Box Office staff to join our free email list. If you would like to be sent a free season leaflet every three months, just include your postal address and postcode.

Follow Us Online

 www.facebook.com/FinboroughTheatre

 www.twitter.com/finborough

Feedback
We welcome your comments, complaints and suggestions. Write to Finborough Theatre, 118 Finborough Road, London SW10 9ED or email us at admin@finboroughtheatre.co.uk

Playscripts
Many of the Finborough Theatre's plays have been published and are on sale from our website.

Finborough Theatre T-shirts
Finborough Theatre T-shirts are now on sale from the Box Office, available in Small, Medium and Large £7.00.

Friends
The Finborough Theatre is a registered charity. We receive no public funding, and rely solely on the support of our audiences. Please do consider supporting us by becoming a member of our Friends of the Finborough Theatre scheme. There are four categories of Friends, each offering a wide range of benefits.

Brandon Thomas Friends – David Alpers. The Beryls. Penelope H. Bridgers. David Day. Mike Frohlich. Bill Hornby. Matthew Littleford. Barbara Marker. Barbara Naughton. Sally Posgate. Michael Rangos. Nick Salaman.

Richard Tauber Friends – James Brown. Tom Erhardt. Richard Jackson. Mike Lewendon. John Lawson. Harry MacAuslan. Sarah Thomas.

Lionel Monckton Friends – Philip G Hooker. M. Kramer.

William Terriss Friends – Leo and Janet Liebster. Peter Lobl. Paul Kennedy. Corinne Rooney. Jon and NoraLee Sedmak.

Smoking is not permitted in the auditorium and the use of cameras and recording equipment is strictly prohibited.

In accordance with the requirements of the Royal Borough of Kensington and Chelsea:

1. The public may leave at the end of the performance by all doors and such doors must at that time be kept open.

2. All gangways, corridors, staircases and external passageways intended for exit shall be left entirely free from obstruction whether permanent or temporary.

3. Persons shall not be permitted to stand or sit in any of the gangways intercepting the seating or to sit in any of the other gangways.

The Finborough Theatre is licensed by the Royal Borough of Kensington and Chelsea to The Steam Industry, a registered charity and a company limited by guarantee. Registered in England no. 3448268. Registered Charity no. 1071304. Registered Office: 118 Finborough Road, London SW10 9ED. The Steam Industry is under the Artistic Direction of Phil Willmott. www.philwillmott.co.uk

UNSCORCHED

Luke Owen

Characters

TOM
EMILY
NIDGE
MARK
SIMON
VOICE
VOICE #2

*Simon and the voices can easily be played by the same person,
so the cast size is five (one female, four male).*

Note on Text

*Any dialogue in square brackets can be omitted, 'swallowed' or
barely spoken. It should not be spoken in full.*

*This text went to press before the end of rehearsals and so may
differ slightly from the play as performed.*

Scene One

An office.

There are two desks, each with a chair and a computer. Connected to each computer are: a mouse, a keyboard, two monitors and a set of headphones.

There is a small kitchenette: sink, cupboards, kettle, kitchen roll, milk (either UHT or in a fridge), sugar, teabags.

There is a small dehumidifier. Its water tank is full.

When the audience is ready:

Music: 'Prelude No. 1 in C Major' – J. S. Bach.

Enter NIDGE *(name rhymes with 'fridge').*

He turns on the main light. He puts down his bag. He switches his computer on. He takes off his coat and hangs it up.

He removes the dehumidifier's water tank. He empties it into the sink. He puts the water tank back into the dehumidifier. It clicks into life.

He sits at his desk.

He picks up a clipboard, attached to which are dozens of printed sheets of A4. He skim-reads. He flicks through a few pages. He puts the clipboard down.

He starts working at his computer.

Seconds pass.

The music ends.

Enter SIMON, *late.*

SIMON. Sorry. Sorry.

NIDGE. 's all right.

    SIMON *sits and switches his computer on.*

SIMON. When's he –

NIDGE. Ten minutes.

Beat.

[What] happened with that stuff from Friday?

SIMON. Finished.

NIDGE. Great.

Beat.

Good weekend?

SIMON. Yeah. Fine. You?

NIDGE. Yeah, [it wa]s all right.

Beat.

You okay to take the first batch?

SIMON. Sure – what is it?

NIDGE. It's, uh, Z492 up to Z499.

SIMON. 'kay. When's it due?

NIDGE. Last Thursday.

Silence.

SIMON *clicks his mouse.*

He hits F8 a few times, annoyed.

He presses and holds his computer's power button. The computer powers down. He presses it again. It whirrs back into life.

's it all right?

SIMON. It's fine.

NIDGE. Might be the damp.

SIMON. Might be.

Silence.

SIMON *presses and holds his computer's power button. The computer powers down. He presses it again. It whirrs back into life.*

Silence.

SIMON *hits 'Esc' a few times*.

NIDGE. [Is it] still playing up?

SIMON. Yup.

Silence.

NIDGE. [Have] you tried Safe Mode?

SIMON. Yes, Nidge, thank you for your input.

Silence.

NIDGE. [Did you] see Helen over the weekend?

SIMON. Have you done something to this?

NIDGE. No.

Silence.

Look, phone Gav.

SIMON. I'm not phoning Gav; Gav's a shit.

Beat.

I don't need Gav.

NIDGE. What's it doing?

SIMON. Just…

Silence.

NIDGE. [Do you] want some tea?

SIMON. No thank you.

Silence.

NIDGE. You okay?

Silence.

Si?

Beat.

SIMON. Hmm?

NIDGE. You all right?

SIMON. [I'm] fine.

Silence.

SIMON *presses and holds his computer's power button. The computer powers down. He presses it again. It whirrs back into life.*

Silence.

NIDGE. Look, [we] might as well get Gav. This 457 stuff, we've –

SIMON. Wait, wait… 457? No. No no no. We finished that. We're –

NIDGE. [We've] had more links come in.

Silence.

SIMON. I'm not doing those.

NIDGE. Si…

SIMON. I'm not. You can.

NIDGE. I am. I'm doing half.

SIMON. How many?

Beat.

NIDGE. Three hundred.

Silence.

SIMON (*devastated*). Right.

Silence.

Mark promised.

NIDGE. But, mate, it's Mark.

Silence.

Let's have a break, yeah? While your computer's loading.

What do you fancy? Buckaroo? KerPlunk? [Or a] bit of Xbox! What's that racing game you like? With the robots.

SIMON *start to cry, silently.*

Silence.

Oh! Hang on. You have to see this. Today's dose of awesome.

He holds up a folder.

(*Mock epic*.) Behold! I present ye: one ordinary-looking folder, identical in shape, size and nature to that possessed by one Mark Hampton. But nay! Gadzooks! Inside: every twenty-third word has been translated into Welsh!

Beat.

Oh, come on, Si – we can do anything! We could go chair racing through the corridors, we could superglue Mark's door shut, we could… we can do literally anything, Si; the world is our oyster and it's a beautiful day.

Silence.

What's up? Si. What's wrong? [I] can't help you unless you tell me.

SIMON. I'm fine.

NIDGE. Okay. Will you help me do the 457 stuff? For me.

SIMON. No.

NIDGE. Si…

SIMON. I can't.

Beat.

NIDGE. You don't really have a lot of choice. [I'm] sorry. Someone has to.

SIMON. Not me.

NIDGE. Then who?

Beat.

SIMON (*gesturing towards* NIDGE). Well…

NIDGE. Would if I could. But… you know, six hundred links…

SIMON. Wait, you mean it's three hundred… each?

Tense silence.

NIDGE *leaps to his feet, energetic*.

NIDGE. Right, sod it, let's play some hangman!

As he writes on an imaginary whiteboard with an imaginary pen:

'kay – one, two, three, four, five, six, seven, eight, nine, ten! Ten letters! Right – first letter!

SIMON. I don't know.

NIDGE. Have a guess. First letter.

SIMON. I can't do this.

NIDGE. Yes you can! Come on, Simon! First letter! What are we saying – 'E' ? Yeah?

Beat.

Right, 'E'!

(*Writing it in.*) Third letter. Last letter. Right! Come on, Si – doing well! Next letter!

Beat.

Next letter.

SIMON. How are you okay?

Silence.

The things we see. How are you not…

Silence.

I mean, look at me. Just fucking look.

Silence.

I can't get rid of this. I can't erase it.

SIMON *cries silently.*

Seconds pass.

NIDGE *takes some kitchen roll from the kitchenette. He walks to* SIMON*'s desk.*

He offers it to SIMON. SIMON *doesn't take it.*

NIDGE *puts it on* SIMON*'s desk.*

NIDGE. What would help? Si.

Silence.

Shall I put some music on?

Silence.

How about some cake, yeah?

Silence.

Or some orange juice? You like orange.

SIMON. [There]'s no orange left.

NIDGE. Lemon, then.

Silence.

I'll get you some lemon.

NIDGE *goes to the kitchenette.*

He makes a cup of lemon squash.

He gives it to SIMON.

Beat.

SIMON *pours it over his monitors.*

Fuck!

A spark and a bang. Blackout.

After a few seconds the emergency lighting kicks in.

Silence.

SIMON. I quit. I quit.

NIDGE *picks up his phone. He presses a button.*

He waits.

NIDGE (*phone*). Hey, it's me. Could you pop through?

Beat.

Uh, no, no, [it] needs to be now. Thanks.

NIDGE *hangs up.*

They wait.

Enter MARK. *He cautiously approaches* SIMON.

MARK. Si?

Silence.

Simon, mate, it's Mark.

Silence.

Just wondered if you fancied popping into my office, buddy.

Just for a bit of a chat.

Silence.

SIMON (*quiet*). Am I fired?

MARK. We just need to have a chat, buddy.

Silence.

SIMON (*quiet*). I'm so sorry.

MARK. I know.

SIMON. I wanted to help people.

Silence.

MARK. Shall we pop through to my office?

Silence.

SIMON. Okay.

    SIMON *starts to get up.* MARK *helps him.*

MARK. Come on, then.

SIMON. I killed my computer.

MARK. That's okay, come on.

    MARK *starts to lead* SIMON *out of the room.*

    (*To* NIDGE.) We'll do our meeting at ten, buddy, yeah?

    Beat.

NIDGE. Sure.

    Exit MARK *and* SIMON.

Scene Two

MARK*'s office.*

MARK *sits alone at his desk, working.*

There is an empty chair opposite him.

Knock knock.

MARK. Come in!

> *Enter* TOM (*mid-twenties*). *He is wearing a suit.*

> *As* MARK *gets up and goes to greet him:*

Tom! Good to see you. Mark Hampton, General Manager.

TOM. Hi.

> *As they head to the seats:*

MARK. [Did you] find it all right, then?

TOM. Uh, yup. Yeah, no problem.

MARK. Great.

> *They are now seated.*

Right! Shoot! Why do you want this job?

TOM. Well my background's always been in IT, and [that]'s great, you know, I love computers, keeping up with all the latest technology… but then I saw this job and I just thought here's an opportunity to put those skills to good use, you know, help fight this sort of crime, just… help people. I guess.

MARK. And that's something that's important to you?

TOM. Absolutely. Yeah, definitely. I wanna make a difference. And I'm really good with SQL, database management, CMS – front end and back end, um… Java, Flash, HTML, Linux, Unix, FTP…

MARK. Bit of an IT whizz.

TOM. I try.

> *They laugh a little.*

MARK. Great. [We] always need that.

TOM. Good good.

Beat.

MARK. Okay, well, [the] good news is: Ruth and the Warner interview guys [were] really happy with your first two interviews – great feedback from those.

TOM. Fantastic.

MARK. Background checks all work out fine, so that's good.

TOM. Great.

MARK. Two more bits we need to do – we've got what we call the image analysis test and then we're on to evidence exposure, 'video one' as we call it, where we'll take you into one of the secure rooms and just… show you a video.

Beat.

TOM. Of the – …

MARK. Well, it's the full gamut, really, right up to what we call 'category five', which is the most serious level of abuse.

Beat.

TOM. Right.

MARK. How's that sound?

TOM. Uh… yeah. Sounds all right, sounds… challenging.

MARK. Oh it is. I mean, don't get me wrong, it'd be completely irresponsible of me to sit here and say it's gonna be a walk in the park. It's not an easy job; some of the things you'd be seeing are… pretty unpleasant. But, if and when you do get to the actual job, we've got a whole load of stuff in place to make sure you're all right – counselling, music, Xbox, and even just stupid stuff, like… Mondays we usually have cake.

They laugh a little.

Away days – [we] went paintballing last year, [that wa]s a good laugh. Free parking – although there's a bit of a… (*Waves his hands slightly.*) thing with parking at the moment. [We've] also just had a big review of all our safeguarding guidelines, so just loads of advice, loads of help, just a really supportive workplace.

TOM. Sounds good.

MARK *takes out a folder.*

MARK. Great! Okay, we'll start with the image analysis. In just a moment I'd like you to open this folder and describe, in as much detail as you think is relevant, the image you find inside.

TOM. Okay.

MARK. Now, I should add: you do not have to open this folder, you can say 'actually, no, sorry Mark I'm not sure I can handle it', [that's] fine. [That's] absolutely fine. But in order for your application to progress any further, we do need to do this.

TOM *looks at the closed folder.*

Beat.

TOM. So you want me to – …

MARK. If that's all right.

TOM. Sure.

Silence.

TOM *opens the folder. He is a little stunned by what he sees.*

Silence.

MARK. In your own time.

Silence.

TOM. Um…

Silence.

Okay. It's a box. Like a plastic… cat box or, kind of carry box. For pets. There's a girl in it. Five, six years old. She's white, brown hair… brown eyes, I think. She's crying.

Silence.

The room's got brown carpet. White-ish walls, kind of that… off – … uh… magnolia. Looks like there's wallpaper, floral print or a branch kind of…

Silence.

She's wet. Like she's… just got out of the bath, [or] something. She's not wearing anything. Her hair's wet.

Yeah.

Silence.

MARK. What else?

TOM. Umm…

Silence.

That's about it. I think. Yeah.

MARK. Okay. Good. Camera flash. Only other thing.

TOM (*closing the folder*). Sorry.

MARK. No, no problem. No problem at all. You did really well. Really really well. Good analytical skills.

TOM. Thanks.

MARK. And they'll only get better.

TOM. 'kay.

Beat.

MARK. How was that?

TOM. Uh…

TOM *laughs a tiny bit, nervously. He is shell-shocked.*

MARK. You okay?

TOM. Yup.

Beat.

MARK. Feel ready to move on to the video footage?

Beat.

TOM. Sure.

MARK. Great. And what I'd say is: after you've seen the video, take the weekend, have a think about it, see how you feel. [Then] I'll give you my direct contact number and we can have a chat on Monday.

TOM. Okay.

Silence.

How do people usually… react to the video?

MARK. Depends. Fair chunk of them don't finish it. Even those who do, about fifty per cent of them then go on to say it's not a job [that] they think could do… and that's fine. Everyone has their limits.

TOM. Right.

MARK. Are you sure you want to do this?

Silence.

TOM. Yes.

MARK. Good man. Ready?

TOM. 's it… in here, or?

MARK. [Uh] no, just down the corridor.

TOM. 'kay.

MARK. Can I get you a glass of water or anything? Cup of tea?

TOM. I'm good, thanks.

MARK. Great.

Beat.

Follow me.

They exit.

Scene Three

Back room of a pub. Speed dating.

EMILY (*early twenties*) *is sitting at a table. She has a glass of white wine. She is wearing a handwritten name badge.*

There is an empty chair opposite her.

A bell rings.

VOICE. Okay, fellas, if you could all move one table round to the right! Thank you!

Enter TOM *with a cider. He is also wearing a name badge.*

TOM. Hi.

EMILY. Hey.

TOM *shows his name badge.*

TOM. Uh… Captain Hook.

As TOM *sits:*

EMILY. Tinkerbell.

They laugh a little.

VOICE. Right! Usual amount of time. Off you go!

A bell rings.

Beat.

TOM. So!

EMILY. So.

Beat.

TOM. How you finding it so far, all right?

EMILY. Yeah, it's all right. You?

TOM. Yeah. Not bad.

EMILY. Cool.

TOM. Cool.

Beat. They laugh a little.

So. Tinkerbell. Tell me about… yourself.

EMILY. 'kay. I… work in a museum.

TOM. Oh right!

EMILY. Yeah, the uh, the Bridger-Cartwright Museum…?

TOM (*hasn't heard of it*). Uh…

EMILY. 's okay. 's tiny, kind of specialist… thing.

TOM. Cool. Enjoy it, or…?

EMILY. I do, yeah; I'm the Education Projects Officer so I deal with getting school trips in, liaising with art teachers, doing guided tours, looking after screaming kids…

They laugh a little.

…stuff like that.

TOM. Sounds good.

EMILY. It is. And the exhibitions they have are, like… wow. Seriously.

TOM. Ah, I shall check it out some time.

EMILY. You should; it's awesome.

Beat.

So. Mister Hook.

TOM. Captain –

EMILY (*smiling*). Captain Hook, sorry. What is it [that] you do, job-wise?

TOM. Uh, I work in digital analysis.

EMILY. Oh wow. So what, like –

TOM. Uh, it's criminal… stuff, basically.

EMILY. Ah cool, okay.

TOM. Although I mean it's not nearly as, you know, as… *24* as it sounds.

EMILY. Still.

TOM. Still. Yeah, no, it's good.

EMILY. You watch *24*.

TOM. I do. I do watch *24*. [Or] watched.

EMILY. Fucking love that show. My ex got me into it; I'm swear he had, like, this man-crush on Kiefer Sutherland.

They laugh.

TOM. Well, he is a fine figure of a man.

They laugh a little.

Beat.

EMILY. I really like your hair, by the way.

TOM. Oh! Thanks.

EMILY. I really wanna touch it. Sorry, [that]'s probably weird of me.

TOM. No, [it]'s fine – you can.

EMILY (*a bit excited*). Can I?

He leans forward slightly.

She touches his hair.

So soft! What do you use, just like [a] normal conditioner?

TOM. Yeah, just… every day.

EMILY. Ha! You're such a girl.

He laughs.

TOM. Thanks.

EMILY (*smiling*). You're welcome.

Beat.

Sorry.

TOM. No, it's fine. Actually I did notice the other day [that] my conditioner says something on it like – (*Advert voice.*) 'Here at Tresemmé we believe that every woman has the right to silky, beautiful hair.'

They laugh hard.

EMILY. Well, I would agree.

TOM. No, me too. Me too.

A happy moment. Silence.

EMILY. Anyway.

TOM. Yup.

EMILY. What was I saying before I was distracted by your silky, beautiful hair?

He laughs a little.

Analysis!

TOM. Yes!

EMILY. What kind of stuff?

TOM. Uh, recorded footage, mainly. [Of] crimes.

EMILY. So it's what, like… CCTV, or…?

Silence.

TOM. Uh, no, it's um…

Uh…

Silence.

I mean it's to do with… it's, uh, child… um…

Silence.

EMILY. Oh.

Silence.

Sorry. I shouldn't have –

TOM. No, it's okay, uh…

Silence.

He laughs a little, nervously.

(*Quiet.*) Shit. [I'm] sorry.

EMILY. No, no no. Don't be silly, why…

A long silence. No eye contact.

VOICE. Okay, you have twenty seconds remaining.

Beat.

EMILY. Twenty seconds.

TOM. Yeah. Um…

A long, uncomfortable silence.

Umm… what do you do for fun?

EMILY. Oh, I read a lot. [I] go to parties with friends, um –

A bell rings.

VOICE. Okay, time's up. Make sure you make a note of your date's name – fellas, if you could all move one table round to the right! Thank you!

Beat.

EMILY. Well, it was nice meeting you. Captain Hook.

TOM. You too, Tinkerbell.

EMILY. Good luck with the job.

Silence.

TOM. Thanks.

Beat.

You too.

EMILY. Thanks. Bye.

TOM. Bye.

Exit TOM.

Scene Four

Music: a soft, slow version of 'Ave Verum Corpus K.618' –
Mozart.

NIDGE *sits alone at a table. He is at home. The room is dimly lit.*

Newspaper is spread out over the table.

An open bottle of beer sits on the table.

He is building an Airfix model. It is an airplane – Spitfire or
similar.

He slowly glues the edge of one part.

He holds it to another part.

He waits.

He gently tugs on the part to see if it has stuck. It has.

He smiles.

He puts the pieces down.

He drinks some beer.

The music ends.

Scene Five

The office.

NIDGE *is working.*

Enter TOM.

NIDGE. Tom!

TOM. Hey.

NIDGE. Good to see ya. Nidge Parrott, Senior Content Analyst.

TOM. Hi.

NIDGE. 's get you started.

   They both sit at SIMON*'s old desk.*

NIDGE *switches the computer on.*

How's it been? [The] HR marathon.

TOM. Yeah. All right.

NIDGE. Boring?

TOM. Uh...

NIDGE. [It]'s okay to say yes.

Beat.

TOM (*laughing nervously*). [A] bit. Yeah.

NIDGE. Excellent. Right – password. Eight characters long, has to have at least one letter and one number.

TOM. Okay.

TOM *types.*

TOM *hits 'Enter'.*

NIDGE. And again.

TOM *types. He hits 'Enter'.*

Fabuloso.

Beat.

NIDGE *picks up a clipboard.*

Right! [The] way it works: we get sent lists of links to investigate. This one's list – (*Reading off the clipboard.*) Z610. Basically all these URLs are websites that either the police or members of the public have flagged up as potentially containing video or photo evidence of child abuse. Our job is to visit these websites, see if there actually is anything suspicious on them – often there's not – if there is we action a report to CEOP – Child Exploitation and Online Protection.

TOM. Right.

NIDGE. Okay?

TOM. Yup.

NIDGE. Right, let's start you off on... (*Looks through his list*.) ah! *Voilà*.

NIDGE *types in a URL, reading it off the clipboard. He hits 'Enter'*.

'kay, so we'll imagine you're going through your working day and this is the first one on your list.

TOM. Okay.

NIDGE. So, as you can see straight away from the video thumbnail it already looks suspicious – you've got the girl there, clearly not wearing a top but we need to go into the video itself and just see what's going on, so!

He clicks.

'kay, so, fairly basic – kids' party, paddling pool – naked children there so clearly this is something the police are gonna want to know about, so! We go into Igloo, which is the software, and you need to log what's going on, brief descriptions of the kids, any adults who are present. Also anything that suggests where we might be – plug sockets, that sort of thing. Obviously in this case we're outside, so. Sometimes I use a dictaphone for all that and write it down later, that's one option... and yeah. Just... visit all these links.

TOM. Okay. Is it just a case of copying them down off the list?

NIDGE. At the moment, 'fraid so, yeah. System's been playing up – ordinarily it's all done with Ignition, this software thing here, but [that]'s been a bit temperamental lately, so... [we're] back on the clipboards for now. [We're] getting it fixed. Supposedly.

TOM. 'kay.

NIDGE. Right, now, this –

NIDGE *double-clicks*.

They wait.

– when it loads...

They wait. NIDGE *makes clicking noises with his tongue*.

...thank you – this is all the missing children in the UK.

NIDGE *starts scrolling through the list.* TOM *didn't expect it to be so many.*

TOM. Right.

NIDGE. [They] get about a hundred thousand a year, and this goes back just over ten years. So. Ones highlighted in green have been found alive, so [that's] most of them. Ones in white are still missing. Ones in red are deceased. Basically, there's another organisation [that it]'s their job to deal with all [of] this, but they've asked us to keep an eye out. [The] basic idea is that if we see any of these kids on any of the websites we let them know but, to be honest... I mean...

They look through the enormous list.

TOM. Sure.

Silence.

Can I just ask...?

NIDGE. Mm-hmm?

TOM. The evidence. How... bad, for want of a better word...

NIDGE. How bad does it get?

TOM. Yeah.

Beat.

NIDGE. Pretty bad.

Beat.

I mean you saw video one, right?

TOM. Yeah, but... I mean, is it all like that?

NIDGE. Oh, no. No. In fact, most of the links we get aren't actually child abuse – often it's adult pornographic actresses who make their living from being... petite, you know? Often it's violent footage that's not against children so that's not within our remit...

TOM. 'kay.

NIDGE. But yeah. You'll get used to it.

Beat.

TOM. Right.

NIDGE. Plus – if ever you're feeling a bit shell-shocked, we've got a whole load of just random daytime TV crap you can watch if you go into your 'Easy Listening' folder here – *Jerry Springer*, *Britain's Got Talent*, bit of David Attenborough, if you're ever feeling a bit worse for wear 'cause you've seen something grim, pop one of those on, take your mind off it for a bit. Or go for a walk, play some Xbox, take half an hour out – [that's] all absolutely fine.

TOM. Right.

NIDGE. Counselling sessions are all paid for, so make use of those… and that's basically it.

NIDGE flicks through the clipboard full of lists.

TOM. So these are all…

NIDGE. This is our 'to do' list.

He keeps flicking through. There are loads.

TOM. And it's just us?

NIDGE. Uh, for this lot, yep. And we get another one of these in every day.

Beat.

TOM. Surely…

NIDGE. Yup.

Beat.

NIDGE offers his hand to shake.

Welcome to digital analysis.

They shake hands.

Scene Six

Speed dating. Different place this time.

TOM *is sitting at a table. He has a glass of wine on the table. He is wearing a handwritten name badge.*

There is a chair opposite him, empty.

A bell rings.

VOICE #2. Okay, next round coming up! Ladies, if you could all move one eligible young bachelor to the right. Thank you.

Enter EMILY *with a beer. She is wearing a name badge.*

EMILY. Oh.

TOM. Ah.

Beat.

EMILY. Captain Hook.

TOM. Actually, it's um – … (*Indicating the name badge.*) Prospero, this time.

EMILY. Beatrice.

She sits.

VOICE #2. Okay! Right! [Your] time starts now!

A bell rings.

Beat.

TOM. Good choice, by the way. [I] love *Much Ado*.

EMILY. Ah, you should have been Benedick.

TOM. I was going to, but it was, uh… [it was] taken.

EMILY. Ah.

Beat.

So you come here as well.

TOM. Uh, well, uh… first time, actually.

EMILY. Mine too. Here, anyway.

TOM. Yup.

Beat.

EMILY. Think we get five minutes here.

TOM. Yeah.

Silence.

How's stuff? How's... how's the museum?

EMILY. Yeah, it's good, just... my line manager's on maternity leave at the moment, so I'm basically doing two jobs.

TOM. Crikey.

EMILY. Yup. So yeah, just... knackered. Like, all the time.

They laugh a little.

TOM. Shit.

Silence.

EMILY. How's – ?

TOM. 's okay. Actually, last week was actually my first day. Speed dating. Uh, the... speed dating last week was right after my first full day of the recruitment... thing.

EMILY. Oh wow, so... first week now.

TOM. Yeah. Yeah.

EMILY. How's it been?

Beat.

TOM. Yeah. Good. I mean... well, the... people seem nice, so...

EMILY. Cool.

Beat.

(*Apologetic.*) Look. About last week...

TOM. [It]'s fine.

EMILY. I didn't mean to –

TOM. Really, it's –

EMILY. I think I might have kinda… freaked out. [A] bit. So…
yeah. Sorry.

TOM. 's okay. Seriously. I mean I know it's not something you
hear every day, you know – 'I work in…'

EMILY *smiles*.

But no, it's fine. Don't worry.

EMILY. Thanks.

Silence.

[I] think it was just surprise, mainly. I mean you seem like
this… cute… nice guy…

TOM. Thank you.

EMILY. Just… how do you wake up one morning and say –

TOM. I dunno.

EMILY. – 'this is what I want to do with my life.'

TOM. [I] don't know.

EMILY. Do you enjoy it? I mean, obviously not the… watching,
but… I mean, job satisfaction, do you – …?

TOM. I guess, yeah, I mean… I wanted to help people. [It's]
like my last job [I] was doing SQL database stuff and it
was… it was all right, it was a living, but at the end of the
day I didn't go home feeling I'd helped anyone. Like, at all.

They laugh a little.

Beat.

And yeah, this job I have now might be tough, or might
mean [that] people react really weirdly to it when I tell them
what I do, but… that's fine. You know? I don't mind that.
[It]'s worth it.

EMILY *understands now. Beat.*

Sorry, [that] probably sounds really wanky.

EMILY. No.

Beat.

[It]'s just your job, at the end of the day. [It's like] my ex was in the army. Plus, I mean… Christ, when people find out a bit more about me they usually run a mile, so…

TOM. Really?

Beat.

Can't imagine that.

EMILY *is flattered but deflects the compliment.*

EMILY. Shut up. [I] could be an axe murderer.

TOM. See, now you're just turning me on.

She laughs a little.

Beat.

EMILY. Anyway.

TOM. Yup.

Beat.

EMILY. What do you do for fun?

They laugh.

TOM. Oh God. I am so sorry.

EMILY. Yup. [It] was pretty awkward.

They laugh a bit.

TOM. Sorry.

EMILY. It's fine. Tell me.

TOM. Tell you what?

Beat.

Oh, what I do for fun! Sorry. I thought you were just –

EMILY. I was.

TOM. Ah.

EMILY. But I actually also wanna know.

TOM. Right. Um…

EMILY. And I swear, if you say anything about computer games –

TOM. B– ...

EMILY. I am walking outta here.

They laugh.

TOM. What makes you think I play computer games?

EMILY gives TOM a look.

TOM tuts and rolls his eyes/similar.

He laughs a little.

Fine.

EMILY laughs.

Um... I bake?

EMILY. Oh for [fuck's sake] –

TOM. What?

EMILY (*laughing*). [You're] such a nancy boy.

TOM (*laughing*). Aw, you're so mean.

EMILY. Ah, you love it. What do you bake?

TOM. Not telling you now.

EMILY. Aww, I was only teasing. Come on, favourite thing. Favourite thing you bake.

TOM (*smiling*). Nope. Don't like you any more.

EMILY. Awww, tell me.

TOM. Nope.

EMILY. Muffins?

TOM. Nope.

EMILY. Cake?

TOM. Nope.

EMILY. Cookies?

TOM. Nope.

EMILY. Brownies?

TOM *is about to say something other than 'nope'.*

EMILY *gasps.*

I am so coming round your house!

TOM. You don't know where I live.

EMILY. Well, I'll just follow you home.

TOM. Okay.

EMILY. And break into your house.

TOM. Okay.

EMILY. And kill you. And eat your brownies.

TOM. Okay.

Beat.

EMILY. You now officially think I'm weird.

TOM. No. Actually I just thought that was hot.

EMILY *laughs a little.*

Beat.

EMILY. You're so strange.

TOM *laughs a little.*

TOM. Thanks.

Smiles. Eye contact. A happy moment.

Beat.

EMILY. So you like theatre?

TOM. Uh… sometimes, yeah.

Contented silence.

EMILY (*happy*). Hmmm.

TOM. What?

EMILY (*blushing/shy*). No, it's…

Beat.

TOM. No, what?

They laugh a little.

EMILY. Nothing.

Beat.

Eye contact.

Eye contact broken. They laugh a little, shyly.

VOICE #2. Twenty seconds, ladies and gents! Twenty seconds.

Beat.

TOM. So!

EMILY. So!

Beat.

TOM. Twenty seconds.

EMILY. Yup.

Silence.

What are you thinking?

TOM. What are you thinking?

Beat. Smiles. A happy moment.

Silence.

They laugh a little.

He tuts.

We're so bad at this.

EMILY. Yup. Sorry.

Beat.

TOM. Okay.

EMILY. Okay. Yes.

TOM. I'm going to go out on a limb here.

EMILY. Please do.

TOM. Would you… like to… do this again some time?

She smiles.

She becomes sadder.

EMILY (*tentative*). Yes.

TOM. But…?

Beat.

A bell rings.

VOICE #2. Okay, that's your lot – ladies, on to your next table – thank you!

Beat.

EMILY. Actually yeah. Yes. I would.

TOM. Sure? You looked like –

EMILY. I'm sure. Nothing too formal, formal sort of… freaks me out, but just… yes. That would be nice.

Beat.

TOM. Cool.

EMILY. Cool.

Beat.

They're both really happy.

TOM. Okay.

EMILY. Okay. Um…

She gets up.

Good to see you again.

TOM. You too.

Beat.

I'm Tom, by the way.

EMILY. Emily.

Scene Seven

NIDGE *and* TOM *working in the office.*

Seconds pass.

NIDGE. How's it going?

TOM. Yeah, 's all right. These ones are all just random bits of TV footage for some reason. If there's anything bad in here it's in like the last few links. So far it's just *EastEnders* and *Supermarket Sweep*.

NIDGE. *Supermarket Sweep*. Crikey.

They laugh a little.

They continue working.

NIDGE *finishes a file and signs it off on his clipboard.*

TOM. How about you, what's your – ?

NIDGE (*heading to the kitchen*). Some guy getting beheaded. Not our remit, though.

Beat.

TOM. Right.

NIDGE. Tea?

Beat.

TOM. Yeah [that]'d be good, thanks.

TOM *clicks another link. He is stunned.*

Beat.

NIDGE. Need more teabags. What do you like? PG Tips? Tetley? Bit of Earl Grey?

TOM *is looking at his screen, petrified.*

NIDGE *sees* TOM*'s screen.*

(*Under his breath.*) Shit.

He comes and sits/stands by TOM.

You remember what to do?

Beat.

Tom.

TOM. Yup. Sorry.

NIDGE. 's okay – pop on the headphones.

Silence.

Mate?

TOM. Uh… s– … um… yup.

TOM *puts the headphones on, one ear uncovered.*

NIDGE. Right, so – notes.

TOM. Yup.

Beat.

NIDGE *waits for* TOM.

NIDGE (*quiet, polite*). You need to write down –

TOM. Uh, yup. Sorry, I – … yup.

NIDGE. 's okay. Right, so. Suspect male, so make a note of that.

TOM *doesn't move.*

Tom?

TOM. Yup.

NIDGE. You okay?

TOM. Yeah, I['m]… make a note of that. Yup.

NIDGE *turns* TOM*'s monitors off.*

NIDGE. Tom, look at me.

TOM *does so and then looks away.*

Silence.

You okay?

TOM. Yeah. Yeah. Sorry, I… yeah, no, I'm fine, um…

NIDGE. 's okay.

Silence.

You all right?

TOM. Yeah, I'm… yeah, no, I'm fine.

NIDGE. Sure?

TOM. Yup.

Beat.

It's just…

Beat.

TOM *exhales, lost for words.*

Beat.

NIDGE. Yup.

Silence.

TOM (*quiet*). What did I just see?

NIDGE. Category three.

TOM. But that was a baby.

Silence.

NIDGE. Look, let's have a break. Yeah? What do you fancy? Bit of *Jerry Springer*? The one with the KKK midgets; literally it's like the perfect episode. Seriously.

Beat.

Yeah?

Silence.

TOM *nods.*

TOM. 'kay.

NIDGE. Good stuff.

TOM. I'm sorry.

NIDGE. No, it's okay. Don't worry.

    NIDGE *takes the relevant sheet off* TOM*'s clipboard.*

    I'll do this one. 'kay? You watch some *Springer*.

    Silence.

TOM. 'kay.

Scene Eight

MARK *working alone in his office.*

Knock knock.

MARK. Come in.

    Enter TOM.

    Tom! Mate! Have a seat, buddy.

    TOM *sits.*

    So! Two weeks. A fortnight, no less. One half of a lunar cycle.

    Beat.

    How's it been?

TOM. Yeah. Fine.

    Beat.

MARK. Good. Good good. Nidge mentioned you had a bit of
a…

    MARK *does a hand wobble.*

    Beat.

TOM. Ah, it was… nothing, really. Just… you know.

    Silence.

MARK. What?

TOM. Oh, just… one of the websites kinda… got to me. A bit.
But, you know. I'm fine.

MARK. Good.

TOM. [I] had a break.

MARK. Great.

TOM. [And I] watched some *Springer*...

MARK. Nice.

They smile.

Beat.

TOM. But then the next link I clicked after that was...

He takes a moment to reflect on the horror of it.

...worse.

Beat.

MARK. How so?

TOM. Just... worse. I don't know, it's...

MARK *waits.*

Weirdly the physical... wasn't as bad. But it's...

A long silence.

(*Slow, sad.*) It's what she says. In the video. This girl in it. What she says to the guy. You know, the guy who's...

Silence.

She says 'I like it when you're happy.' And she's smiling, and... and she keeps saying it: 'I like it when you're happy.' Over and over again. And she's like... five. And he's...

Silence.

MARK. It's okay, buddy.

Silence.

TOM. And [it] sounds stupid but there's this like... classical music. In the background. 'cause she's like a ballerina or something, um...

Silence.

And she dances… ballet… before it all happens and there's like this classical music on in the background and – (*Laughing a little, sadly*.) [it] sounds stupid but the same music's on this car advert on TV at the moment and I just know at some point tonight I am gonna be watching TV and that… (*Laughing a little, sadly*.) fucking advert's gonna be on and I am gonna be… a mess, basically. Um…

Beat.

And I don't know what to do about that.

Beat.

Sorry. [I] shouldn't have sworn.

MARK. [It]'s okay.

Silence.

Is there anything we can do to help? You've got your contact phone numbers in case –

TOM. Yeah, no, no I've got that.

MARK. Okay.

Silence.

Would you like to take maybe an hour out? Or go home, or –

TOM. I'm okay.

MARK. It's no problem.

Silence.

TOM. I wanna keep going.

Silence.

MARK. Okay. When's your first counselling?

TOM. Uh… [it] was meant to be today but I didn't. I didn't go.

MARK (*reproachful*). Tom.

TOM. I know.

MARK. You have to –

TOM. I know.

Beat.

MARK. Have they rebooked something for you?

TOM. Not yet.

MARK. Right, well I'll drop them an email.

TOM. Okay.

MARK. Why didn't you go?

Beat.

I mean, you know it's free, right?

TOM. I know. I know, and that's great, thank you, but... I don't want to have to walk into a room and have to talk about it. You know? I'd rather just try not to think about it at all, outside work.

MARK. Tom.

Silence.

Look, I'm sorry to be the heavy on this, but I need to know that you're gonna go to your next counselling. Otherwise I can't –

TOM. Okay.

MARK. – I can't keep employing you; it puts you in breach of contract.

TOM. Okay.

MARK. Plus if you don't go, I get it in the neck from upstairs, I have to give you a verbal warning – I'd just rather not have to go down that route.

TOM. Okay. I'm sorry.

MARK. No, it's okay. It's okay, buddy. Just... we're trying to help you.

Beat.

TOM. Okay.

Silence.

MARK. So you'll go.

TOM (*unsure*). Yup.

MARK. Good man. Top stuff. Bloody contracts, eh?

TOM *smiles politely.*

Beat.

Other than that, though?

Beat.

TOM. Fine.

MARK. Good.

Beat.

Good. Main thing to remember: we are all here for you.
You've got me, you've got Nidge, you've got counsellors –
great counsellors… everyone's rooting for you, buddy;
everyone's here to support you.

Beat.

TOM. Thank you.

MARK. No, no problem. No problem. I'm always here. My
door is always open.

Scene Nine

Night. EMILY*'s studio flat. Artsy and tiny.*

Sofa bed (currently in sofa mode).

Snacks. Two wine bottles – one empty, one half-empty. Two half-full glasses of wine. Bag of weed. Ashtray. Lighter. Rizlas. Tobacco. Box set of 24 DVDs.

EMILY *and* TOM *are sat on the floor.*

They are quite drunk/stoned.

EMILY *is rolling a joint.*

EMILY. 'nother episode?

TOM. Can do. In a bit.

EMILY. Cool.

TOM. See, this is the problem with *24,* you feel you have to watch it, like –

EMILY. Back to back.

TOM. Yeah.

EMILY. I did that.

TOM. Really?

EMILY. Mm-hmm. Season one. But then it's only, like, eighteen hours because each episode is only forty-five minutes 'cause of the ad breaks, so you end up [with] like, six missing hours and you're like… whaaat? Why do I have extra hours in my day? Who put them there?

TOM. 's where all the leap years go.

Beat. EMILY *laughs.* TOM *laughs.*

EMILY *(still laughing).* What?

TOM. I don't know; sorry – that made more sense in my mind than on my… in my…

EMILY. Mouth?

TOM. Yes. Thank you.

Contented silence while EMILY *finishes rolling.*

She holds up the joint.

EMILY. Ta-da!

TOM. Yay.

They laugh.

EMILY. You are so baked.

TOM. I'm not, I'm just nicely…

EMILY. You're a baked potato.

TOM *giggles, stoned.*

TOM. Baked potato.

EMILY *giggles, stoned.*

Contented silence.

EMILY. Do you think the FBI has, like, a set work rota?
Because surely he's technically working illegal overtime if
he's working for twenty-four hours without a break.

They reflect on the thought.

I'd lol so fucking hard if, like, the first eight episodes were
just him asleep.

They laugh hard.

TOM. And then the ninth was him hitting snooze, like, 'fuck
this shit' –

EMILY. – like, twelve times.

TOM. Yup.

They stop laughing.

Beat.

EMILY. So. Mister Lake.

TOM. Just realised I don't actually know what your surname is.

EMILY *(emphasis on the second syllable)*. Clemmell.

TOM. 'Clemmell' . Awesome.

EMILY. I hate it. Everyone pronounces it wrong.

TOM. Least you didn't use to get called 'Gayke' .

EMILY *laughs*.

EMILY. 'Gayke'. 's clever.

TOM. Yup.

Beat.

EMILY. Sorry.

TOM (*not offended*). 's fine.

EMILY. [I] bet you were in the chess club. Like, captain of the chess team or something.

TOM. Nope. Orchestra, though.

EMILY. Ahh.

EMILY *briefly studies* TOM.

Clarinet.

TOM. Trombone, actually.

EMILY. Oh. You look like a clarinetist.

TOM. [And] what does a clarinetist look like?

EMILY. You.

Beat. TOM *laughs a little. A happy moment.*

TOM. So. Miss Clemmell.

EMILY. Mister Gayke.

TOM *tuts/rolls his eyes/similar, much to* EMILY*'s amusement.*

TOM. Orchestra? Chess? What was your –

EMILY. Ballet, actually.

TOM. Oh right. Any good?

EMILY. Got up to grade four. And I was only about eleven when I took that, so…

TOM. Crikey.

A long silence. No eye contact. TOM *is lost in thought. About work.*

EMILY. You okay?

Beat.

TOM. Knackered.

EMILY. Well, it's like… gone midnight.

TOM. Shit.

EMILY. Yup.

Silence. Their faces are very close.

TOM. What time do you have to be up?

EMILY. 'bout… seven thirty? Eight?

TOM. Cool.

Beat.

EMILY (*smiling*). Why?

TOM *shrugs*.

TOM. Just… curious.

Beat.

They laugh a tiny bit, nervous.

EMILY. 'kay.

TOM. 'kay.

Slightly awkward silence.

[I] should… probably think about… making a move.

EMILY (*smiling*). 'Making a move'?

TOM. Uh, well, I mean, like… you know. Heading… home. You know. Offwards. In an… offward direction.

They laugh a little.

Silence.

Although it's pretty comfy here.

EMILY. It is.

TOM. Could totally just like… fall asleep here.

EMILY. Well, this is where I sleep, so…

TOM. You sleep on the sofa?

EMILY. 's a sofa bed.

TOM. Oh! So's that… not another room, then?

EMILY. Nope, that's the airing cupboard.

TOM. Ah.

They laugh a little.

Sorry.

EMILY. 's okay.

Fixed eye contact. Their faces are very close. Silence.

TOM. So.

EMILY. So.

Silence.

TOM. Do you want a hand? With the… sofa bed, I mean. Turning it into… um… you know, turning it into a…

They are looking straight at each other.

Beat.

EMILY. Bed.

TOM. Bed.

Fixed eye contact. Silence.

EMILY. Can do. Sure. Although you don't have to, I mean I can –

TOM. No, it's fine.

EMILY. [I've] got it down to a pretty fine art, so…

TOM. No, it's okay, [I] don't mind.

Fixed eye contact. Silence.

EMILY. 'kay.

TOM. 'kay, um…

Beat.

They get off the sofa bed.

(*Instructing him.*) Okay, if you uh…

TOM. Yup.

EMILY (*instructing him*). And then –

TOM. Got it.

They fold out the sofa bed.

They stand either side of it, looking at each other.

Silence.

EMILY. Thanks.

TOM. [You're] welcome.

Silence.

So, um… I guess I'll see you at the weekend, or…

EMILY. Yeah, no, definitely.

Silence.

Did you have, like, a jacket or – …

TOM. Uh, no, just… as is.

They laugh a little.

EMILY. Cool.

TOM. Cool.

Beat.

(*Indicating the exit*). So um…

EMILY. Yup.

They head towards the exit.

She opens the door.

They stop.

Beat.

TOM. [I] had a really nice time tonight.

EMILY. Me too.

Silence.

Fixed eye contact.

Suddenly they move in to kiss each other.

They clash teeth/lips. Hard.

Ow, fuck, ow!

TOM. Shit, ow! Sorry – you okay?

EMILY. Shit, got my –

TOM. Yup.

EMILY. – lip on my… teeth and…

TOM. Sorry. Shit, ow.

Beat.

EMILY. You all right?

Beat.

TOM. Yup.

Beat.

You?

EMILY. Yup.

Silence.

Suddenly they both laugh. It goes on for some time.

TOM. Shit.

EMILY. Yup.

They stop laughing. They smile.

They laugh a little.

They embrace.

They look at each other.

A happy moment.

TOM. You okay?

EMILY. Yup.

They laugh a little.

Silence.

TOM. [Shall we] try that again?

They smile. They kiss. She swings the door shut.

They continue to kiss.

Scene Ten

The office. NIDGE *and* TOM *working at their computers.*

Seconds pass.

TOM. Nidge?

NIDGE. Mm-hmm?

TOM. [You] got a sec?

NIDGE *takes off his headphones.*

NIDGE. Yup.

TOM. Bit of a random one – just gonna send you a link; let me know when it comes through.

TOM *clicks or hits 'Enter'.*

'kay, right, [that's] sent.

Beat.

NIDGE. Got it. D'you want me to –

TOM. Yes please.

NIDGE *clicks.*

NIDGE. Right.

TOM. So – ten images. Girl. Probably about seven, eight?

NIDGE. I'd say nine or ten.

TOM. Cool. But… category one.

NIDGE. Yup.

TOM. So I've put it under 'of interest'.

NIDGE. Mm-hmm.

TOM. But! 'kay, see at the bottom of that page there's a tiny tiny bit of text.

NIDGE. 'Copyright 2009, all rights reserved.'

Beat.

Huh.

TOM. Exactly! Weird, right?

NIDGE. It is.

TOM. I mean I've never seen a –

They laugh a little.

NIDGE. No.

TOM. – copyright thing on a –

NIDGE. Yeah, no. Doesn't happen.

TOM. Exactly – that's what I thought. So. Hover over that.

NIDGE. What –

TOM. Where it says 'all rights reserved'.

NIDGE. 'kay.

TOM. The 'v' in 'reserved'.

NIDGE moves his mouse.

Beat.

NIDGE is amazed.

(*Smiling.*) Click it.

NIDGE clicks. He looks, amazed.

NIDGE (*flabbergasted*). What?

TOM. It's a message board.

NIDGE. Yeah, no, totally!

TOM. Like a forum or something.

NIDGE. Yeah yeah, definitely. '*Sueños de la juventud*' – what is that, Portuguese?

TOM. Spanish. [I] looked it up, it means 'dreams of youth' .

NIDGE *gives* TOM *a look*.

(*Excited*.) I know, right? And I can't find any record of this forum ever being reported or looked into or anything – not here, not [in] Spain, South America, just nowhere. No one seems to know about it. I mean, I can't get into it 'cause it's all bloody passworded and locked up like Fort Knox but look at how active it is, you can see –

NIDGE. 4:01 p.m. GMT, that's like… ten minutes ago.

TOM. Exactly.

NIDGE. Oh, mate.

TOM. So yeah. Just… thought you might like to know.

Beat.

NIDGE. Wow.

They laugh a little.

TOM. So what do we do?

NIDGE. Right, yeah, let's get report actioning! So, international one, so if you go to INHOPE 'Notice and Takedown'…

TOM (*doing so*). 'kay.

NIDGE. And then just fill in the details, URL, how you found it, what you found… and when you're done hit 'send'.

TOM. Great!

NIDGE (*optimistic*). And then… who knows?

TOM *smiles and nods*.

TOM. Who knows?

Beat. They laugh a little.

Beat.

NIDGE (*getting up, heading to the kitchen*). Right! I think that calls for a celebratory Wagon Wheel.

TOM. [Let]'s do it!

They laugh a little.

Beat.

NIDGE. Nice work, mate. Seriously nice work.

TOM *smiles*.

Scene Eleven

The office. Empty.

The door is unlocked.

Enter TOM. *He switches a light on.*

He opens his desk drawer. He looks inside it.

He tuts/sighs.

He looks around.

He heads to his coat, which is still hanging up.

EMILY *appears at the doorway.* TOM *doesn't notice.*

TOM *searches his coat pockets. He takes out his phone. He is relieved to have found it.*

He notices EMILY.

Beat.

EMILY. Find it?

TOM. Coat pocket.

EMILY. Told you.

TOM (*smiling*). Yup.

She comes in, but only as far as the kitchen area.

She looks around.

What do you think?

EMILY. Looks nice.

Beat.

Surprisingly.

They laugh a little.

She looks around for a bit but doesn't touch anything.

She spots an A4 printed sign in the kitchen. She laughs a little.

Who's Mark?

TOM. Uh, he's… General Manager – why?

EMILY (*reading it*). 'This kitchen is a privilege not a right, please keep it tidy at all times', double underlined.

They laugh.

He sounds fun.

TOM. Yup.

They laugh a little.

Beat.

(*Suggesting that they go.*) Shall we…?

EMILY. Wow, you have CDs; do you listen to music?

TOM. Not often.

She looks at the CDs.

Beat.

EMILY (*laughing*). Ha! You have Simply Red in here. [What] the fuck?

They laugh a little.

TOM. Not mine.

EMILY. Right.

TOM. 's not.

EMILY. Yup.

They laugh a little.

Silence.

(*Smiling.*) You okay?

TOM *thinks about it.*

TOM. Yeah. Actually. Happy.

She comes over to him. They embrace.

She looks up at him.

EMILY. Well, good.

They kiss.

I like it when you're happy.

TOM *is suddenly uncomfortable; it's what the girl in the video said.*

He retreats from her.

Silence.

TOM. What?

EMILY *doesn't understand. Beat.*

EMILY. I like it when you're happy. Why, what's – …?

An awful silence.

TOM. Shall we, um…

He gestures towards the exit.

Neither of them moves.

EMILY. What's wrong?

TOM. No, nothing. Just…

Beat.

…worried we're gonna miss our reservation.

Beat.

EMILY (*unsure*). Okay.

Silence. Neither moves.

TOM. Shall we…

Beat.

He heads towards the exit.

She follows.

He opens the door.

He exits.

Beat. She is worried.

She follows.

Scene Twelve

Music: 'Everyday 2.0' – Carly Comando.

NIDGE *sits at home. Dim lighting.*

Newspaper-covered table. As before.

A beer is on the table. Half-empty.

He picks up the complete but unpainted AirFix Spitfire.

He smiles.

He takes out a small paintbrush. He takes out a small paint pot. Using a screwdriver, he prises the top off it.

He dips the paintbrush into the paint and begins to paint the airplane.

The music ends.

Scene Thirteen

MARK*'s office.*

TOM *is slumped in a chair. He is a shattered wreck.*

Silence.

MARK. I would urge you to reconsider.

TOM. I just don't think I can do this any more.

MARK. What part of it is it that's upsetting you?

TOM. It's having to watch child abuse all day.

MARK. But you knew that was part of the –

TOM. I know. I know.

   Silence.

MARK. Think back to when you first applied for this job. What
was it that drew you to it?

TOM. I don't know.

MARK. I think you do.

   Silence.

TOM (*quiet*). I wanna help people.

MARK. Well that is exactly what you are doing, Tom. Every
single day.

TOM. But –

MARK (*picking up the phone*). Look, let's get Nidge in.

TOM. No, look –

   MARK *presses a button.*

MARK (*phone*). Mate, it's Mark; could you pop by? Cheers,
buddy.

   He hangs up.

   Silence.

   Enter NIDGE.

NIDGE. Yup?

MARK. Nidge, me ol' mucker. Come in, come in.

NIDGE. [I'm a] little bit busy, Mark...

MARK *takes* NIDGE *to one side*.

MARK. Tom's thinking of leaving us. Just hoping you might be able to talk him round, impart some of the ol' Parrott wisdom.

NIDGE. [But] if he wants to quit, he should just quit.

MARK. Oh come on, mate, that's not the attitude, is it?

NIDGE. Mark, two words: Simon Carter.

MARK. That's not gonna happen again.

NIDGE. I'm not doing this.

MARK (*so* TOM *can hear*). So, Nidge, you think Tom should stay?

NIDGE *isn't happy. Beat*.

NIDGE (*louder, deadpan*). Definitely, matc. One hundred per cent. He should absolutely stay; that is in no way a bad idea.

Beat.

MARK. Thanks, Nidge. That'll be all.

NIDGE. [I] could say more if you want.

MARK. No, that's been great. Thanks.

NIDGE. Good good.

Beat.

(*To* TOM.) Take care, mate. 's been a pleasure.

Exit NIDGE.

Beat.

MARK. Okay. Fine. You wanna leave, I'm not going to stand here and stop you. But this job, you have a real opportunity to get down there with the scum of the Earth and make a difference. I envy you actually, Tom.

TOM. You wouldn't. Not if you saw what I've seen today.

MARK. Tell me what it was that upset you so much.

TOM. I can't. [It] wouldn't be fair.

Silence.

MARK. When's your next counselling?

TOM. Thursday.

MARK. Right, well… let's leave it till then, yeah? And we can see how you feel then.

Silence.

What have you been on today?

TOM. Fours and fives. Mainly.

MARK. Well, mate, that's why! I bet even Nidge fancies quitting right about now.

Silence.

You'll get used to it. I mean, look at Nidge.

Beat.

Oh! Completely forgot to say! 'Dreams of youth' forum. [The] one you found. Turns out it was a new one; they hadn't spotted it before. Argentinian.

Beat.

TOM. Wow.

MARK. I mean, we haven't had any more information than that just yet, but my guess – how these things usually work – is that they're now monitoring it, waiting to swoop in, make arrests, press charges, take children out of harm's way.

Silence.

TOM. Huh.

MARK. So yeah. Nice work.

TOM *is proud, exhausted and moved by it all. It almost brings a tear to his eye.*

Silence.

And that is why you're here.

Silence.

Scene Fourteen

EMILY*'s flat, night. It is empty. The sofa bed is still in bed mode.*

Enter TOM *and* EMILY, *drunken and giggly.*

They stagger into the flat. She shuts the door.

They kiss, drunk and passionate, as he takes her coat off.

EMILY. Mmm.

They kiss.

TOM. What?

They kiss. She giggles.

EMILY. Nothing. Mister fuckin' heroic.

They giggle.

TOM. [I'm] so not.

EMILY. You so arc.

(*Playfully.*) Shut up.

They giggle.

They kiss. They kiss more.

*She grabs his belt and pulls him closer towards her.
They kiss.*

He kisses her neck.

They stumble slightly. They giggle.

He slips off his shoes and nearly loses his balance.

They laugh.

*They kiss some more, taking more clothes off and heading
towards the sofa bed.*

TOM. Just gonna nip to the bathroom quickly.

EMILY. 'kay.

Exit TOM.

EMILY *hurriedly tidies a few things away.*

She turns a side light on and switches the main light off.

She takes a compact mirror out of her bag and checks herself in it. She puts the mirror back in her bag.

She sits on the edge of the bed.

Enter TOM.

TOM. Hey.

EMILY. Hey.

She pats the bed.

They laugh a little.

He comes and sits next to her.

Happy silence.

Do you want a drink?

TOM. I'm okay.

EMILY. 'kay.

Happy silence.

She pokes his shoulder.

They laugh a little.

He suddenly grabs her and climbs onto her. She squeals slightly and giggles. They are both smiling.

They kiss. They take off more clothes.

As they kiss:

Mmm.

TOM. What?

EMILY. 's nice.

They laugh a little.

They kiss some more.

(*Playful, seductive.*) Guess what I did.

TOM (*grinning*). What?

EMILY. Feel.

She takes his hand. She slides it slowly up her leg. Further and further up.

TOM. Shaved your legs.

EMILY. Well, yes, but…

She guides his hand further up.

(*Quiet, seductive*.) Not just my legs.

TOM *freezes and retreats very slightly.*

Silence.

TOM. Think I might have a drink.

Beat.

EMILY. Okay.

He goes off to the kitchen.

EMILY *sits up. She is a little worried.*

She waits.

[There's] cold ones in the fridge.

TOM (*off*). Thanks!

She waits.

TOM *reappears with a can of slightly fancy cider.*

He sits down next to her.

He doesn't open the can.

Silence.

EMILY *strokes his shoulder. He doesn't look at her.*

Beat.

EMILY. You okay?

TOM. Yeah. Yeah yeah.

Silence.

She kisses him.

Silence.

Bit tired.

Silence.

EMILY. Oh.

TOM. Sorry.

EMILY. No, it's fine. [It]'s not like it's mandatory…

They laugh a little.

TOM. I know, but –

EMILY. Just… thought it might be nice. What with our being all… official and stuff.

TOM. I'm sorry.

EMILY. No, it's okay. Don't worry.

Silence.

TOM. Thanks.

They smile.

They kiss and hold on to each other, tenderly but not sexually.

Silence.

EMILY. You okay, though?

TOM. Yeah. Yup.

They kiss.

EMILY. Good.

Silence.

Scene Fifteen

The office.

TOM *and* NIDGE *working.*

Silence.

NIDGE. You all right? Quiet today.

TOM. Yeah, no, just… deep in thought.

NIDGE. Ooh, don't wanna be deep in thought here, mate. Bad idea.

   TOM *laughs a little.*

   NIDGE *ticks off a list on his clipboard.*

TOM. Any good?

NIDGE. Seen it before. Old category five.

   NIDGE *gets up.*

   Tea?

TOM (*sad*). I'm good, thanks.

   NIDGE *looks at him.*

NIDGE. You all right?

TOM. Yeah, just… lots going on.

NIDGE. Wanna chat?

   TOM *smiles but shakes his head.*

TOM. I'm all right. Thanks.

   NIDGE *starts making tea.*

   Seconds pass.

NIDGE. How's things going with your lady friend – what's her name?

TOM. Emily.

NIDGE. Emily.

   Beat.

   Going well?

TOM. Think so.

NIDGE. Great.

Silence.

TOM. Can I ask you something?

NIDGE. Mm-hmm?

TOM. How long did it take you to get used to…

NIDGE (*indicating his computer*). What, the –

TOM. Yeah.

Beat.

NIDGE. Dunno. A while?

Beat.

I mean for ages I still used to get pretty shook up if I'd seen a four or a five – that took a while to go…

Beat.

Why?

TOM. Just… [I'm] finding it easier to watch the… stuff than when I started.

Beat.

NIDGE. Great.

NIDGE *continues making tea.*

Beat.

TOM (*unconvinced*). Yeah.

NIDGE *continues making tea.*

Seconds pass.

But I mean you've just sat there and watched a category five.

NIDGE *stops making tea but doesn't turn to face* TOM.

And now you're having a cup of tea.

NIDGE. But that's my job.

TOM. But don't you feel bad about that?

NIDGE. Why?

TOM. Well, I mean maybe this stuff should upset you. Us. These days I watch a category one or two and it barely even registers. And I don't understand that, I don't...

Beat.

It's like last week. After all those fours and fives. Next one on my list – [I] clicked the link and it looked like it'd only be a two so I thought 'fine, let's get through this, let's get home, let's... spend time with Emily, get pissed, watch *South Park* and go to sleep.'

Silence.

And I load the video up – last one of the day – and I hit play and bang, we're straight in. The crime is going on. [It's] there. Straight away. And my first thought, when it started, wasn't 'oh God, how awful', you know, 'that poor kid, what the hell's he doing to him,' it was...

Silence.

...it was about the blanket. On the bed. Sonic the Hedgehog. And I thought 'oh, I used to have that blanket.'

Silence.

And I spent... five seconds, maybe, my mind wandered and I thought about that blanket and wondered what happened to it and whether it was probably in the attic at my mum's house and then suddenly I realised 'I am thinking all this while I am watching a child being abused.'

Silence.

And I finished that link and I moved on to the next one, and that was easy, just some guy filming kids in the bath. But that sort of stuff used to upset me. And now it doesn't.

NIDGE (*sympathetic*). But that's a good thing.

TOM. Is it, though?

NIDGE. Course. [It's] distance. You don't stand in the middle of a fire to put it out, do you? You step back.

TOM. But I feel like a bad person. It's like I don't care or
something.

NIDGE. But everyone does this, mate. You see on the news [that]
eight people died in a landslide in Brazil or wherever and you
think 'shit, that's nasty – wonder if [*The*] *X Factor*'s on.'

TOM. But that's awful.

NIDGE. But everyone does it. And it's not because you're a bad
person, it's just because you don't know those people. And
you don't know these kids. Neither of us do.

TOM. But it's child abuse. Surely that's –

NIDGE. But it works on the same principle. Eventually.
Everything does.

TOM. Even child abuse?

Beat.

NIDGE *nods, sadly.*

NIDGE. Yeah.

Silence.

[I] thought you said you were finding it easier.

TOM. But maybe I should be upset. Maybe my heart should
feel bruised. Maybe I should cry. I mean, surely someone
should.

NIDGE. But that's what the public do. If they wanna cry, if they
wanna get upset – fine. But we're not here to do that, we're
here to help.

TOM. But I still want to feel that pain; I need to.

NIDGE. But you won't survive that way.

Silence.

(*Kindly.*) Look. Look, I've seen a lot of people sit in that
chair while I've sat in this one. And the biggest mistake
people make is that they care; they grieve for every child
they see getting abused so they never stop grieving and it
just messes them up.

Beat.

This job needs to be done, you know – and you can't survive in it if you care. People think you can. They think 'oh, you can still care a little bit.' No. Trust me. If you care, it will kill you. You take that little bit of caring, that little bit of compassion, that little bit of allowing yourself to get fucked up by what you see and you multiply it by – (*Indicating the computer or clipboard.*) that…

Beat.

That'll kill you.

Silence.

TOM. When did you stop caring?

Silence.

NIDGE (*quiet, sad, distant*). [A] long time ago.

Beat.

TOM. And are you okay with that?

Silence.

NIDGE (*quiet, distant*). Course.

Scene Sixteen

EMILY*'s flat. The sofa bed is still in bed mode.*

EMILY *is sat on the bed, working on her laptop. She is exhausted. She is wearing a dressing gown over cartoony penguin pyjamas.*

Knock knock.

She smiles and gets up to answer it.

It's TOM.

EMILY. Hey!

TOM. Hey!

They kiss. They hug. They stay hugging for a little while.

She sighs a little, exhausted.

You okay?

EMILY. Yeah, just... stupid museum stuff.

They kiss.

They sit on the bed.

Just gotta finish one email and then I am all yours.

TOM. 'kay.

Beat.

EMILY (*working*). How's work?

Beat.

TOM. Fine.

EMILY. Cool.

TOM. Yours?

EMILY. Ugh. Melinda is doing my actual head in. Motherhood has just like... I swear she's about one step from licking a napkin and wiping my face with it.

TOM *laughs a little.*

She keeps working. Seconds pass.

D'you wanna pop the TV on or something?

TOM. I'm okay.

EMILY. 'kay. Literally twenty seconds. Promise.

She reads. He waits.

She clicks/hits a button.

Done!

She closes the laptop.

Sorry.

TOM. 's okay.

EMILY. You all right?

They kiss.

TOM. Mm-hmm.

EMILY. Cool.

TOM. Cool.

Beat.

EMILY. What do you wanna do?

TOM. Dunno. What is there?

EMILY. Well! We could…

As she speaks she climbs onto him, straddling him and touching his chest.

…watch *South Park*, or we could get stoned, or we could…

(*Flirtatious, taking off her dressing gown*.) …think of other things to do, um…

They laugh a little.

TOM *sees the penguins on the pyjamas and is uncomfortable.*

They kiss.

She slides her hand down his chest.

She kisses him.

She starts to slide her hand into his trousers.

TOM (*stopping her*). Um…

She stops.

Beat.

EMILY. What?

TOM. Can we…

It's clear that he wants her to get off him.

She gets off him.

A long silence.

Sorry.

Silence.

EMILY. Okay.

Silence. As little eye contact as possible from here onwards.

(*Worried.*) We could... watch a movie, or something?

TOM. Can do.

EMILY. If you like.

TOM. [I] don't mind.

Silence.

What do you wanna do?

EMILY. Well...

She laughs a little, bitterly.

TOM. Right. Sorry.

A long silence.

EMILY. Are you having second thoughts? About –

TOM. No.

Silence.

EMILY. 'cause this keeps happening.

Silence.

Is it that you don't fancy me any more?

TOM. No.

EMILY. Then what?

A long silence.

TOM. Shall we do something else?

EMILY. What have I done?

TOM (*frustrated*). Nothing, just...

Silence.

EMILY. Are you okay?

Silence.

I want you to be okay.

TOM. Everyone says that.

EMILY. Well I do.

TOM. Okay. Okay.

Silence.

EMILY. But this keeps happening. Like that time at your office or after the meal thing… you suddenly get all upset and I don't know why and suddenly everything's ruined and I don't even know what I've done.

TOM. You haven't done anything.

EMILY. Then what just happened? Why have I just made an idiot of myself trying to have sex with you when you're clearly just completely uninterested?

A long silence.

TOM *(quiet)*. Why are you wearing penguin pyjamas?

EMILY *now understands what's wrong.*

Silence.

EMILY. So you don't want me to wear the pyjamas.

TOM. But I can't be one of those guys who dictates what you can and can't wear. I'm not some sort of controlling arsehole.

EMILY. But if it's going to upset you – …

TOM. But it's up to you; you should be able to wear whatever you want.

EMILY *(almost laughing)*. But it's just PJs. It's fine; I'll get new ones.

TOM. But it's not just the PJs.

Silence.

It's like… I dunno, like the teddy.

EMILY. What teddy?

TOM. The… you know, the – elephant… thing. In the corner.

EMILY. Mister Snuffalump.

TOM. Right. I mean, does he have to be there?

EMILY. Well… no, but…

Silence.

So Mister Snuffalump is upsetting you.

TOM. No, I –

EMILY. But that's what you're saying.

TOM. Okay. Fine. Yes. Fine. Mister Snuffalump is upsetting me. But I can hear how stupid that sounds. It's stupid, I just –

EMILY. It's not stupid, I just need to know this stuff! You don't tell me. And then you fucking freak out because I've said or done or worn the wrong thing somehow and I'm meant to know what's going on – well I don't!

TOM. Well, it's fairly simple, just don't behave like a fucking child!

An awful silence.

I mean I'm sorry but you can't expect me to want to be sexual with you if you're wearing fucking Pingu pyjamas or whatever. I mean can you not see that that's gonna be a problem?

An awful silence.

EMILY. Right.

Silence.

So you don't wanna be a 'controlling arsehole' , but you're now telling me –

TOM. I know.

EMILY. – what I'm allowed to have in my flat, what I'm –

TOM. Just forget it.

EMILY. – allowed to wear –

TOM. Look, just wear whatever you want!

EMILY (*bitter*). Oh well thanks, Tom. That's great. Thanks – [I'm] glad I have your permission.

A long silence.

Do you still want to be in this relationship?

Silence.

TOM. Course.

EMILY. But you had to think about it.

Silence.

TOM. I don't wanna keep arguing.

EMILY. Well neither do I. But if you're not going to talk about what's upsetting you...

TOM. It's work.

EMILY. Right, well, I figured –

TOM. Right.

EMILY. – that part out.

TOM. Okay.

Silence.

EMILY. You need to talk to me about this stuff.

TOM. Why does everyone want me to talk about it, though? I don't want to talk about it. It's fucking horrible.

EMILY. But look at what it's doing to you.

TOM. But I'm coping.

EMILY. Are you?

Silence.

TOM. I'm just stressed. It's a stressful job.

EMILY. Yeah, but I get stressed too.

TOM. [That]'s different.

EMILY. I know. I know it's different but it's still stressful, and actually you help me with that. But with you I just feel useless, it's like you won't let me help – you won't let me in.

TOM. You don't want to be let in.

EMILY. Because I'm not strong enough.

TOM. Because no one is.

Silence.

I mean, [you] go through life thinking that there's a limit to the things that people will do to each other. But there's not. There's just not.

A long silence.

EMILY. I'm really worried about you, Tom.

Silence.

I wanna help you.

Silence.

TOM. How?

Silence.

EMILY. I don't know.

Silence.

I don't know.

TOM. I don't think you can.

Silence.

EMILY. [I'm] starting to agree.

Silence.

Scene Seventeen

Music: 'Ballade No. 1 in G Minor, Op. 23' – Chopin.

NIDGE *sits alone at a table. The room is dimly lit. Newspaper is spread out over a table. There is an open bottle of beer.*

The Spitfire has now been painted.

He wets a transfer sticker and applies it to the airplane.

He waits for it to dry.

He pushes it to see if it has dried.

It has.

Seconds pass. NIDGE *stares into space, holding the airplane.*

He looks at the airplane.

Seconds pass.

Calmly, he puts the plane down on the table.

He exits.

He comes back on carrying a metal bin. It is full.

He stands in front of the table.

In a sudden burst of movement, he slams the bin down on top of the airplane.

And again.

And again.

And again.

And again.

And again.

He lifts up the bin. The airplane is shattered.

He drops the bin on the floor.

He knocks over the beer bottle. Beer washes out over the table.

Exit NIDGE.

Scene Eighteen

The office.

MARK stands alone.

Enter TOM. *He is tired.*

MARK. Mister Thomas Lake Esquire.

TOM (*he's late*). Sorry.

MARK. 's all right; [you're the] first in.

TOM *looks at* NIDGE'*s desk.*

Beat.

TOM. 's he all right?

MARK. Traffic, probably. Or he had to give his missus a lift.

TOM *didn't know* NIDGE *was married.*

Beat.

TOM *sits at his computer and switches it on.*

Beat.

Can't log in till he's in the building, I'm afraid.

TOM. I know.

MARK. Them's the rules.

TOM. Yup.

They wait.

MARK. Oh [we've] got a Fun Day next week. Go-karting.
Should be a laugh – [you] up for it?

Beat.

TOM. Uh… sure. Yeah.

MARK. Good man. [I'll] drop you an email. And at some point
I'll need to have a word about [your] probation.

Beat.

TOM. Three months.

MARK. Nice one.

TOM. Thanks.

Enter NIDGE. *He hasn't slept.*

MARK. [Th]ere he is! Man of the hour! You all right?

Beat.

NIDGE. Never better.

MARK *hands* NIDGE *printed sheets of A4.*

Thanks.

MARK. Ten minutes?

NIDGE. Yup.

MARK (*exiting*). Have a good day, buddy.

NIDGE. You too…

Exit MARK.

(*Quiet, bitter*.)…buddy.

Silence. NIDGE *isn't making eye contact.*

TOM. You all right?

Beat.

NIDGE. Rough night.

TOM. Wanna talk about it?

NIDGE *smiles slightly.*

Beat.

NIDGE. I'm okay.

Beat.

NIDGE *switches his computer on and sits as he talks:*

You okay to take the first batch?

TOM. Sure, what is it?

NIDGE. It's AA005 up to AA025.

TOM. Cool.

NIDGE. See Emily over the weekend?

TOM. Uh actually that, uh… that ended.

Beat.

NIDGE. Shit. [I'm] sorry.

Beat.

TOM (*sad*). 's okay.

Silence.

Just one of those things.

Beat.

NIDGE. You'll be all right.

TOM. I know, [I] just…

Silence.

[I] hope she is.

Beat.

NIDGE. She will be, mate. Don't you worry.

Beat.

TOM *nods slightly, unconvinced.*

Beat.

Music?

TOM. Sounds good.

NIDGE *hits a button. Music: a soft, slow, piano-only version of Schubert's 'Ave Maria'.*

Nice.

NIDGE. Bit'a Schubert. [The] guy was a dude.

TOM *smirks a bit.*

Seconds pass.

Ready?

Beat.

TOM *inhales*.

He exhales.

Beat.

TOM. Yup.

They each put on their headphones – one ear uncovered.

They start working – watching, typing, clicking.

They continue working.

Lights fade out very slowly.

When the lights are out, the music comes to an end.

Curtain.

A Nick Hern Book

Unscorched first published in Great Britain in 2013 as a paperback original by Nick Hern Books Limited, The Glasshouse, 49a Goldhawk Road, London W12 8QP, in association with Papatango and the Finborough Theatre

Unscorched copyright © 2013 Luke Owen

Luke Owen has asserted his moral right to be identified as the author of this work

Cover image: © Diane Diederich
Cover design: Ned Hoste, 2H

Typeset by Nick Hern Books, London
Printed in Great Britain by Mimeo Ltd, Huntingdon, Cambridgeshire PE29 6XX

A CIP catalogue record for this book is available from the British Library

ISBN   978 1 84842 369 5